Angel Chimes

Angel Chimes

Poems of Advent and Christmas

Judith Sornberger

Shanti Arts Publishing
Brunswick, Maine

Angel Chimes
Poems of Advent and Christmas

Published by Shanti Arts Publishing
Interior and cover design by Shanti Arts Designs

Shanti Arts LLC
193 Hillside Road
Brunswick, Maine 04011
shantiarts.com

Cover image by Lorenzo Lotto, *Angel Annunciating*.
1527. Oil on panel. 29.5 x 21.6 inches (75 x 55 cm).
Church of Sts. Vincent and Alexander, Ponteranica,
Italy. Wikimedia Commons. Public Domain.

Interior images: [stars used throughout] istock.com/
Ekaterina Romanova; [10] istock.com/gerisima; [12] istock.
com/cjmckendry; [29, 81] Father John B. Giuliani and
used with his permission; [38] istock.com/Juanmonino;
[64] istock.com/cstar55; [69] *The Child* copyright
© 2014 Janet McKenzie www.janetmckenzie.com

ISBN: 978-1-951651-61-9 (softcover)

Library of Congress Control Number: 2020949481

For my "sisters"
Jennifer Maatsch (in memory),
Jill Mickel,
and George Doug Shipley,
for all our Christmases.

For Karl Schneider,
who has often been mistaken for the jolly old elf,
with love.

Contents

Holy Family

Acknowledgments

Grateful acknowledgment is made to the editors and publishers of the following journals and books where these poems first appeared:

Bones of Light (Parallel Press): "Preparations"

Dear Winter (Northwoods Press): "Angel Chimes"

Ekphrasis: "Annunciation of the Nahuatl"

The Hard Grammar of Gratitude
(an internal chapbook published in *Poems & Plays*):
"Forest Creche without People"

hidden manna: "Annunciation"

I Call to You from Time: "Mary Muses on the Missing Portrait," "Madonna of the Wheat," "Mary Ponders the Nature of Free Will," "Grace," and "As It Is in Heaven"

Open Heart (Calyx Books): "Stained Glass"

Poems & Plays: "Mary, After the Angel"

Practicing the World (Wipf & Stock): "Silent Night"

A heart full of gratitude to my *anam cara* and writing partner Alison Townsend for inspiration, encouragement, and help with these poems.

Thanks to Lilace Mellin Guignard for our writing retreats, friendship, and help with these poems.

Thanks to Christine Cote for her beautiful attention to this book and in all things published by Shanti Arts.

Thanks to my late parents, William E. Mickel and Roberta Mickel, for giving me and my sisters such loving and abundant Christmases.

Thanks to my late husband, Bruce Barton, for his sensitive and loving comments on some of these poems and for sharing the writing life with me for over thirty years.

Angel Chimes

In a few days Christmas will descend
on them, bearing the usual burden
of breakable wonder, but tonight
she and her sons will walk to the store
to buy candles for the angel chimes.

When they return to their dark house,
they will awaken the Christmas tree's
blinking eyes, take turns lighting
the slim white candles. And she,
who no longer believes, will believe
anything this close to Christmas.

The angels will wear the offering
of light upon their wings.
They will follow one another
around the central star
in a circle born entirely of light.

The song of their turning
will tingle over the woman's skin.
The children will be silent,
turning in their own orbits.
This close to Christmas
she will believe
they will never turn away.

Preparations

Annunciation

All over Florence angels make announcements
they have made for centuries to Marys
holding poses no one would believe.
But finally I find you here—
as the angel found you—slumped on a stool,
pulling into the cave of yourself, hands
crossing: two wings over your belly.
You don't have your finger in a book,
pretending nonchalance when he shows up
in gold-embroidered robes and wings
still dripping rainbows.

Not like those staged rendezvous:
Gabriel bowing suitor-like,
offering his nosegay of white lilies;
Mary a coy courtesan decked out
in her best dress and diadem, knees
saying no-no as they sashay
away from his honeyed words,
torso swaying into his advances.

It's not his rosy finery
I can't turn away from.
It's the stunned yes
of your face I recognize.
I have sat as you do in this portico,
knowing I could answer yes or no.
And I have passed through the pillars
of this archway, praising the great
wisdom of the body.

Oh, but how I envy you this moment:
knowing the world will never be the same,
still innocent of how your world will change.

✳

*from the fresco by Fra Angelico
in the Cloister of San Marco (page 17)*

Fra Angelico (1395–1455)
Annunciation

fresco
Convent of San Marco
Florence, Italy

Mary, After the Angel

What has he left her
but this puzzled profile,
these arms wooden

with wonder, this window
that holds neither
moon nor star,

this dove she pulls
into her girlish midriff,
hands crossed like waiting

wings across its breast,
cradling the fierce
pulse of the future.

✳

from *Transformations: Looking to the
Future with Dove* by Carol Mothner

Annunciation of the Nahuatl

This Gabriel creeps in from the dark
like a husband late returning
from the secrets of the lodge.
Crowned with a longhorn skull,
robed in another creature's skin,
perhaps he still believes he has a mission
as he shuffles toward the light she embodies.
She leans into the gold adobe wall,
belly bulging in her soft white gown
beneath the full moons of her breasts,
already dreaming her child into being.

Her head tilts back so shade and light
can carve her face into the sharp
contours of knowing everything
he might attempt to tell her. *Fear not*,
he whispers, and her hawk's eye opens,
but not to him. It's gliding up
and inward, as if to seize an older,
deeper current, and a tiny smile
edges toward laughter. For his words
are swallowed by the song of all creation
swirling through her, through the unborn
one's feathery motions—
a duet that no angel can enter.

✳

from the painting by Jose Chavez Morado

Preparations

for Janice

Thirty-six and not a son
or daughter to her name.
Does she want one?
Her mother told her
angels bring us babies.
In her dreams they flew through sunrise,
pink and blue tufts streaming from
their icy morning wings.
Aunt Jenny had no children.
Didn't the angels like her?

She lifts crystal angels
from a tissue paper cradle,
arranges them under this year's
Christmas tree—a tumbleweed.
Yes, she is tumbling, drifting . . .
Wasn't there something
she wanted to ask for?

She sets up the papier-mâché creche
next to the angels, like dolls
under the tree, a new baby each year,
the way she thinks it must be
for women without choices.

Has she made a choice?
Or is she waiting for someone
with a beautiful name like Gabriel
to tap her on the shoulder?
She wraps the tree in white
lights and tinsel like a bride.
All night it will say "O"
in the black window.

Down-home Annunciation

Girl, I can't believe you don't look up
as the falling angel bounces and crashes
through the branches of the apple tree
in your backyard, shrieking, *Hai-ai-ai-ai-ail,*
Mary, the Lord is with thee.

You're hanging out the faded rainbow of your laundry,
hens gossiping and pecking near your slippers,
and, for a moment, when he's hit earth, you mistake
the sunrise tatters of his wings for a dropped nightgown.
Then they flutter and he rises from beneath them,
starts his spiel—*Blessed art thou*, he says,
waggling his shaggy eyebrows, *among women*—
pretty close to lines you've heard before
from all the guys who think they are God's gift.

Still, something in his unlaced boots, his not
quite handsome grin, makes you invite him in
for coffee, even though the trailer's kitchen
barely holds the watercolor wings
that, like a hyper hound, won't settle down,
that shimmer with a light that looks like wind.

You've never been the easy kind, but by the time
you've hit the grounds at the bottom of your mug,
even though you still don't know his name
or why you are the winner of the sweepstakes,
you've bought the story anyway—
lock, stock and barrel-sized belly.

❋

from Julie Vivas's illustrations in *The Nativity*

Our Lady of Lunacy

Was she crazy to say yes
when the angel came knocking
at her door? God, yes.
But think about it.
You're a teenage girl opening
the door, and here's this hunky
stranger saying you've just
won the lottery of God's love.

Forget your mother's warnings
once upon a time. You're letting him
in, doing your best to ignore
the neon wings he's jamming
through the doorway and the way
they stir things up once they're inside.

Not to mention the strange new light
that follows him in, pulsing so brightly
you completely lose your bearings.
All you can do is say yes and yes
and yes as if some crazy waltz
is having its way with your heart.

But skip ahead.
This is a cautionary tale.
The word yes so often
gets a girl in trouble.
No matter how they spin it,
you will end up weeping.
So our mothers warned us.

God knows, their job is to keep us
from danger's touch.
But God's job is to make us dance
in languages we can't understand.
To make us big with something
we can't help turning over
our very bones and teeth to,
something that will tear us open,
make us love beyond all reason.

Mary Visits Her Cousin Elizabeth

Gabriel may have had the patter
and the courtier get-up, but
if there's a love story in this gospel,
surely it is here—in these braided
women wrapped in blankets, holding
one another before a backdrop
of cloud bellies nearly as full
of promise as theirs.

Mary's arms support her older cousin's
stooped back and shoulders. Elizabet's
hand lights like a brown dove on scarlet
stripes running down Mary's belly,
while her other palm reaches up
to cup the younger woman's cheek.

Why are we given this image
of these two, belly to belly—
knowing what they knew of God
and what's to come via the wisdom
of the body—when it isn't central
to the bigger picture: divine plan
meets willing human heart?

Overhead their gold orbs converge
into a heart-shaped sun, as though
two women might be needed, after all,
in telling the fullness of God's love.
Perhaps they stand here not only as mothers
of God and his prophet, but also as mirrors,
magnifiers of each other's stories.

�֍

from the Native American icon painting
by Father John B. Giuliana (page 29)

~ 27 ~

Father John B. Giuliani
Mary Visits Her Cousin Elizabeth

MARY VISITS HER COUSIN ELIZABETH

MARYSH ISAHKAATE ELIZABETH KUSSASHBILEELIK

O, the Blessed Privacy of Women

Here they meet like comrades
plotting revolution, and who,
besides their handmaids, notices?

Leaning into one another,
they're two wings of a dove
that will, in due time, lift off,
pulling the whole world with her.

Right out in plain sight
two gold leaf discs start spinning
above their modest headcloths,
but the guys loitering nearby
turn their backs and gawk over
the wall. One dandy flatters
another, and the world spins on.

Do I hear in their deep gaze
the laughter of two women
with a secret—a belly laugh
to rock the unborn infants
whose lives, in this embrace,
they link forever?

A few among their retinue
are shaken by the tremor,
hands flying up in wonder.
Perhaps the others recognize them
as two among the multitudes
of women who pull off the extraordinary
each day without drawing notice or envy.

Think of Emily, of Georgia, think of Zora—
how down to earth they seemed. Think of Sexton and Kumin,
how from the beginning each knew what was in the other,
how they brought it forth together.
How they flew.

✳

from the fresco *Visitation of the Virgin to
Saint Elizabeth* by Domenico Ghirlandaio (page 33)

Domenico Ghirlandaio (1448–94)
Visitation of the Virgin to Saint Elizabeth

fresco
Tornabuoni Chapel in the
Church of Santa Maria Novella
Florence, Italy

Grace

for Jamie

No doubt you'd recognize
this old gentleman. He hangs
above many a faithful table,
his creased forehead leaning
into the gnarled nest of folded fingers,
grateful for the crumbs of life—
the humble loaf, the bowl of soup
waiting near his elbows, light seeping
from an unknown source above him.

When my son found him
a few days before Christmas,
propped against the dumpster
outside the apartment
he rarely leaves, he wondered
how anyone could abandon him there
and brought him inside,
happy to offer him a *proper home.*

That's how my son is, you see—
recognizing a life
where others see an object.
Maybe he gets it
from his crazy mother
who believes God
leaves us such windows.
Or maybe it's this season
when we yearn to shelter
whatever comes knocking
in whatever shape it appears.

✳

from the colorized photograph by Ernest Enstrom

The Recipe Book

She stands at her table,
finger on the tattered page,
the way Gabriel finds Mary
in Renaissance paintings.

Who knew we could be
so lovely in a kitchen
washed by snow light?

Milk in a small glass pitcher,
eggs dreaming in a basket,
and above the woman's pink apron,
a pinch of creamy cleavage.

Light licks the inside
of the blue ceramic bowl
she's braced against her
belly, the better to mix
the gathered ingredients.

Who knows what Mary is reading
when the angel interrupts her?
Does her finger follow
an ancient narrative of making—
handed down mother to daughter,
spattered with secrets sacred as scripture?

✳

from the painting by NC Wyeth

Silent Night

Incarnation

for Jill

"The Word became flesh and
pitched his tent among us." (John 1:14)

Setting out the tiny figures,
fragile as a newborn's first breath,
I recall the year, decades ago,
my sister sent them to me
when I was a single mother—
alone and scared as Mary
must have been after the angel—
wondering how I'd pay
December's heat bill, let alone
create my sons' Christmas.

It seems a miracle
this blended family of angels,
shepherds, kings, lambs and oxen
has survived so many upheavals,
illnesses and deaths of my beloveds,
still encompassing the kneeling couple.

I place the naked infant
at their center, his arms reaching
up like tendrils of flame
from a small fire that beckons
us to warm our hands, to camp
within its glowing circle
on this brief night of our earthly sojourn.

Zebra at the Manger

How did I arrive at this birth, and why?
The sheep followed the shepherds,
camels carried kings, even chickens
have lived here since their hatchings.
Yet we're all carved from the same tree—
one that doesn't grow where my kind roam,
a place that's just a dream—a tale
of swaying grass, a weave of herds—
whispering a child deep into sleep.

Does this child wonder why he came here?
Do the stars of his native place pulse
still behind his clenched eyes?
Was I placed above his makeshift crib
so that, when he wakes he'll see
a creature alien as he? Will the sight
of my stripes give him comfort,
make him giggle, make him less afraid
to be a stranger?

✳

from a wooden nativity

Peruvian Crèche

I'd be content without a wise man,
an angel or a shepherd before I'd relinquish
creatures huddled round the naked infant.
Isn't the warmth of grass-sweet breath and fur
a greater gift than anyone else offered?

And would the story of this moment
have lived on if not for their sacrifices—
quill pens whittled from their feathers,
vellum scraped from their young hides?

And where would we have found words
without birds, beetles and serpents
who inhabited the ancient alphabets
before they evolved into abstractions?

Reasons enough, I suppose, for their admission,
but not why I revere the shaggy sheep
and llama, natives of the mountaintop
where they were formed from clay.

Without an ear twitch or a murmur
they say *it happened here.*
It happens everywhere: the Word
entering the world each day.

But wait. There is a bear—
an animal unknown to those mountains.
So how did she arrive here with the others?

Unless she's Ursa Major,
shedding luminous skin for thick black fur,
padding down the night sky,
crossing borders, centuries and stories
to bear blessings to all Her children.

Sandro Botticelli (1445–1510)

The Mystical Nativity

The Mystical Nativity

If I lift my eyes one moment
from the axis of Mary's adoration,
I'm dizzy on the carousel of winged
and twirling chorus girls above her.

From the wings of the homespun spectacle,
angels point like carny barkers,
cajoling artless shepherds, even wise men,
to step right up: seeing is believing.

It's a miracle that Mary
doesn't shush us or look ruffled.
Perhaps her cloak's a hooded cave
whose silence she retreats to
each time we gather in this vertigo
of gimmicky rejoicing.

❋

from the painting by Sandro Botticelli (left)

Papier–mâché Crèche

Mary and Joseph are doll actors
in a pageant, solemn in the spotlight,
pudgy cheeks flushed with the import
of this moment. The wise men grasp
like birthday guests the gifts
they'd rather not relinquish: vials
of frankincense and chests of gold.

They don't know how fragile they are:
just flour-paste and paper.
Don't know they're only children
trying to do the work of grown-ups.
In early days a husband brought these
figures to me when I was round with child.
We didn't know it's not enough to kneel
before the mystery, to feel delight.
Now our sons fly back and forth between us
trying to heal what has been broken.

Maybe if Mary keeps her eyes closed
her child won't grow
out of his straw-filled cradle,
and she won't wear regret
like a veil over her halo.
Maybe she and Joseph won't
snarl at one another, or if
they lose their heads, God's super
glue will put them back together.

Maybe she will never
doubt God's mercy.
Maybe if she keeps
her plump palms pressed
together, none of us will
have to know the future.
Maybe a child will save us.

A Carol to Mary in Mid-December

My twins have nearly reached the age
of your son when he left you, yet the flame
of dim December as it burns to embers
ignites the memory of our birth-givings.
Especially this night, here in hills swaddled
in snow and fawned over by the moon,
I need you near me as I hear again
The twin musics of joy and sorrow
singing in each woman who delivers
new life to this planet—the bass
and treble clefts of loving children.

According to the wise men's prophecies,
my preemie sons weren't supposed to live,
yet they labored to bring forth each breath
until the night a white flurry of nurses
proclaimed the miracle of their survival.
Yet, as you learned years after steering
your son home from Egypt, one night's reprieve
leads to the next day's mourning.

One calls to say he and his girlfriend
have started looking for a house.
We don't mention his little boy
living far away now with his mother.
As I lay the phone down in its cradle,
my other son rings with the news
that his beloved has left him.
When his voice cracks, I can do nothing
but relive my body's tearing to release him.

No wonder I am most at home
singing carols set in minor keys—
"O Little Town of Bethlehem,"
for instance, where our hopes
and fears are next door neighbors.

Forest Creche without People

Who knows if they are waiting—
two tiny deer and their carved fawn
posed before the grass-filled manger,
the squirrel and rabbit crouching
under whittled pines? And, if so,
what kind of savior do they pray for?

Do they, who never flipped
a white tail in the face of the Creator,
require a miraculous reunion?
If their kind's sole fall has been
beneath the pounce of predators,
from what do they need redeeming?

Maybe the manger's green
is no nest for god or babe,
but the only grace these folk crave—
miracle enough in this season
of dark hunger, prayer enough—
their bowing to receive it.

Christmas Portrait

How soon a girl must learn
to turn her arms into a cradle—
hands grasping one another
to keep the blonde bisque
doll from falling—years before
she'll waken to a stain crimson
as this morning's Christmas frock.

One day *Mutter* will tell her
of the body's mysteries
and what's to come, but today
the girl will marvel
at the Christkind's arriving
in the night to leave this gift
while she was sleeping.

The girl's pink feet dangle
from the straight-backed chair
where she poses, rose lips prim,
dark brows drawn into a slight frown
as if pondering her duty
as *mutter* to this precious
and precarious beauty.

❉

from Gabriele Munter's painting *Girl with Doll*

Silent Night

for Bruce Barton (1953–2012)

Every carol this December
sings your silence as I drive
the icy roads we used to sing on
to distract ourselves from danger,
taking turns choosing the tunes
till we ran out of verses.

Or until your reedy voice cracked
on a high note (or emotion) and,
embarrassed, you'd start replacing
sacred words with naughty ones.
It came upon a midnight clear,
I'd begin, and you'd follow,
that glorious dong of old.

Or you'd start, *Angels we have
heard when high,* and I'd refuse
to go on till you promised
to sing straight. But during

"The First Noel" you'd wander
off again, a wayward lamb,
to certain poor shepherds
who *lay humping their sheep.*

You are going straight to hell,
I'd giggle. You never stopped,
even when our headlights
illuminated storms of swirling stars
and I begged you to pull over.
Maybe you knew
you wouldn't die that way.

Alone on a cold winter's night,
swaddled in the whispering
heat of our all-wheel-drive,
I'm no longer terrified
of icy roads. In fact, I'm almost
hoping that one of these nights
I'll spin off in your direction,
singing *Sle-ep in heavenly piss.*

Mary Ponders the Nature of Free Will

Your hands know nothing
but tenderness, yet your eyes
slide away from the child
on your lap picking each bead
of blood from the pomegranate
resting in your palm.

Brows arch above your hooded eyes
like wings that would fly
to another story. Old eyes,
these, in such a lineless face.
Eyes that know what's going on
behind your back, behind the whirring
blade of your halo.

It's like a little factory back there:
Reach back and up and you can almost
touch your mother propped against
her pillows after childbirth,
handing your swaddled body to a servant,
her fingers reluctant to leave
the blonde fur of your cheek,
as though they fear the fate
they give you to.

A few steps farther back and up,
she greets your father, pulls him
upstairs through the doorway
of the room where she'll conceive you.

Do you wonder, my dear,
when the angel came to your door
that ordinary morning, if, eons before,
he had squinted through the keyhole
of this split-level story, glimpsing
this trinity of scenes?

Were you already seated
in the foreground of this tondo
before he knelt, wings throbbing
in the charged air between you?
Before he called you lucky girl
and reached into the perfect, pressed
folds of his robe to release the white bird?
Pages and pages before you whispered,
Let it be so.

*

after *Madonna with Child* by Filippo Lippi (page 57)

Filippo Lippi (1406–69)
Virgin with the Child and
Scenes from the Life of St Anne
(Tondo Bartolini)

Galleria Palatina
Florence, Italy

Mary Muses on the Missing Portrait

A pregnant woman
understands Eternity—
never quite believes
the days of dreaming her child
into breath will end.
Until they do.

My child was baptized first
in his mother's waters.
I hold it still
the holiest of washings.
They say I felt no pain
when my body split,
that I remained unbroken.

Where were those Fathers
when I told Joseph
stop the donkey now,
water spilling between
my legs: a revelation.

Where are the portraits
of that moment?
Giotto, Rembrandt, Titian—
you with all your genius
couldn't see it.

Not even Artemisia,
both mother and painter,
caught me falling to my knees
in hunched wonder.
Even she would not deliver
my writhing to the canvas:
the second when I knew
the angel had been true.

What else but God's arrival
could occasion such a starburst
of brute straining? Why has no one
painted that epiphany across my vision?

Christmas Eve

for Karl Schneider

Driving to your hand-built house deep in the woods,
I'm wishing for a ring—a star-like stone to lead us
to a new life together after the death of my husband
and the loss of your long-time love. Dizzy from following
taillights through the swirling snow, I enter the glow
of your kitchen, the heavenly scent of baking bread.
Pulling a Santa hat over your long white hair,
you say, *I've often been mistaken for the jolly old elf.*

Before I take off my boots, you want us to crunch
through the snow to your workshop, to show me, you say,
the new toy you bought yourself. I'm thinking
it's some fancy tool or gadget. But just inside the door

stands my mother's drop-front secretary we brought
back from my sister's barn in Kansas—broken by time
in the years since Mom died—the red desk that lived
in our kitchen, witness to every meal she cooked us.

Now here it is, whole again, and painted a scarlet
deep as my mother's kiss, bronze handles gleaming
from your caress. I almost fall to my knees
in wonder at her presence in this chilly outbuilding.
I can't imagine wishing for anything else—not the past
for all its sweetness or the baubles of the future—
only this moment and to kiss you, so I do.

December 26

My dear, you look anything but merry
beneath your circlet of barbed holly,
even though you're the picture of plenty—
pears and pomegranates spilling
between your knees, a gleaming ring
of keys braceleting one wrist
to open the kingdom or the pantry.

One arm cradling a decked out, glowing fir,
the other circling the child who occasioned
all this fuss, this mess—the over-
flowing box of baubles at your feet
beside the dripping bowl of cookie dough,
the greeting cards yet to be addressed,
the mandolin and score of *Silent Night*
for the caroling you've yet to organize.

I suppose you imagined your yes
was a once in a lifetime deal,
never guessed you'd birth this monster
of a season, dooming and—yes, blessing, too—
the women of your line to heavy labor.

I admit each year I buy it, too,
fall for the glittering angel's seduction,
for silent babies, stars and cozy mangers
on the cards I truly mean to send.

Amnesia veils my head and shoulders
like a snowy mantle, like the one
falling on women after they deliver
so we will go on falling on our knees
in fresh wonder, saying yes and yes
and yes, till we find ourselves one morning
gazing off into the distance, stone-faced
with exhaustion, blinking our eyes, frantic
to get out from under all this favor.

❋

from *Christmas Madonna*,
a Christmas card painting by Edward Hays

Holy Family

The Child

For once, Mary, you're not left
alone holding the babe
after the hoopla's over—
Joseph returned to his workshop,
shepherds to their flocks,
wise men to wandering under stars.

Someone finally recognized
you'd crave your mother's witness
to the infant's beauty and a pair
of tender hands to pass
him to in weary moments.

Your face and your mother's
hover like dark moons
over the tiny bundle—white
as the lily Gabriel offered—
in which a child must breathe
though we can't see him.

But what child does the artist
call us to behold? Perhaps you,
barely a teenager? For, though
we grow beyond our mothers' cradled
arms, aren't we eternally their children?

Or perhaps the younger sister,
grasped by your mama's hands
as if she hopes to hold her to this moment—
the girl's hands turned upward,
but still empty of the future,
though a red receiving blanket
rests across her forearms.

This child's somber eyes
pour their dark light into ours
as though she aches with the weight
of your burden, as if begging to be
spared such an immense
and terrifying blessing.

❋

from the painting by Janet McKenzie,
featuring Mary, her mother, and a younger girl (page 69)

Janet McKenzie
The Child

Hanumas

for Cathy Kushner

Of course, we adored our sons, but we weren't madonna-type moms.
Nights when they stayed with our exes, we dated, or danced
to bluegrass in bars and went home with cute guitar players.

One Saturday, we took the Y's parenting class, mostly for the free
childcare, allowing us to go out for lunch. To introduce ourselves,
each woman—it was all women—wrote a word describing herself

on her name tag. Later, over soup and salad, we laughed at
being the only two to choose *intelligent* when all else
were *loving, nurturing,* and *kind.* Such rebels!

That year we launched our small crusade to cobble together
Hanukkah and Christmas. Wishing to show our sons
the seamlessness of what is sacred, we gave birth to Hanumas.

Always there was the miracle of light in deep December—
at your place, the kids with solemn faces took turns lighting the Menorah;
at mine, they lit tapers to fuel the angel chimes' turning.

The night flared into joy and laughter as they hung sequined
pine cones on the tree at my house and decorated snowman cookies,
spun dreidls, and peeled foil from chocolate Hanukkah geld at yours.

Do you recall a single strategy they tried to teach us at that class
for raising good and happy children? Me neither. God knows,
we screwed up plenty. But didn't we do a few things right?

In these dark days, I recall the candles we set glowing on those evenings,
how love wed to intelligence can beget enough light to let us see
there is a flame burning both within us and beyond us.

✻

after stabbings in a rabbi's home during
a Hanukkah celebration, December 28, 2019

Blessed Are the Poor

Each Christmas he's born again in my mind—
the child who'll one day be a student
in my poetry writing class. It's early December,
and the lesson is memory—using details
and quotations to write of family holidays.

After writing awhile, a few of his peers
read aloud of the fragrant Christmas tree,
glittering gifts, and Grandma's turkey.
Something like that. I really don't remember.

Too cool, or too shy, to raise his hand,
he lifts an eyebrow—a sign I've learned
to read as willingness to speak. Each year
now he's the Wise Man bearing the gift
I don't want to open or sing about, but must,
as I recall his poem—his memory

of one year in the projects—
Mama dragging home from work
Christmas Eve, making cocoa,
passing out cookies her lady sent
home, getting crabby when he turns
on the TV to a stupid holiday movie
where everyone gets what they want.

In the morning when there are no presents,
he tells himself he will not cry. He will
not cry. Is he saying this to himself now
as he reads about his mama saying Santa
didn't come "cause you were bad"?

The room has never been so silent.
No one knows what to say,
who to blame, or what to believe
in anymore. Which is one gift,
I suppose, a poem can leave us.

Stained Glass

for my sister, Christmas Eve

One of Michael's windows hangs between us
and the darkness, its one red eye a blind clot.
  You're telling me your recurring dream:
the bell rings; through the storm-door's glass
he proclaims himself alive, his drowning a lie.
  His blood, he promises, still courses
through his body, connecting all his organs,
  like the leading in his windows, holding
  colored shapes to his design. His face
  has all its color. You believe him.

  Your face drains with the telling.
From his sleep your son sends up a whimper,
  like a bubble bursting on the surface
  of the pond his dad went under.
Each time you try seeing Michael's face now,
  you're straining through the muddy
  moss-strewn water, a pane so opaque
  no light will travel through it.

His paid work was restoring churches' windows,
  putting back a fallen halo, replacing
  the cracked pink feet of apostles.
While he made them whole, did he believe them holy?
  Now is the darkest time,
  the season for believing.

As the candles sputter toward extinction,
we borrow phrases from the speech
you gave your son before the funeral,
try mixing them with splinters
of carols he sang this evening.

The stars are brightly shining.
But they are far away, too far
to give us new light in this lifetime.
We say someone so *tender and mild* must be,
though we can't see him, shining somewhere.

But no light solders cut glass over your head
into an aureole as confirmation.
The blues, gold, and the roses
his hands joined are joined to darkness.

As I put the tapers out, you tiptoe
to where your boy lays down his sweet head,
and though we cannot say we know
the stars look down where he lies,
God rest you, sister, in this brief absence
of color; and tomorrow, for the child's sake,
let nothing you dismay, though memory takes
its diamond blade across your face,
and each smile you make is a crack
beginning.

Villanelle in Snow Time

Snowfall is the season of deep sighs—
a time designed for retracing our tracks
or for getting lost in a surmise.

A woman recalls her infant's cries—
her hand falling softly on its back.
Snowfall is the season of deep sighs.

Every snowflake whispers *hushaby*
while constructing quiet's habitat,
inviting us to enter its surmise.

Stillness wakes more memories. They lie
in jagged pieces—fallen bric-a-brac.
Snowfall is the season of deep sighs.

Will they fit back together? You can try,
hoping that the missing ones you lack
may be found in silence's surmise.

Or look out on the snow, and rest your eyes
on white's creation of a world intact.
Snowfall is the season of deep sighs.
Let yourself fall into its surmise.

Sisters, Sisters, There Were Never Such Devoted Sisters

If my sisters and I were Alcott's little women,
our cousin Dougie was Laurie—
partner in all fun and misdemeanors.
Our moms never knew who to blame
when an underground newspaper turned up
in one of our rooms or they overheard us
singing the Doors' or Stones' sexy lyrics.

Whose idea was it for us to perform
the "Sisters" number from *White Christmas*
for our church youth group's Christmas program—
Dougie dressed in drag like Bing and Danny Kaye?
All we remember is giggling and singing, *Caring,*
sharing every little thing that we are wearing,
as we dressed him—like a linebacker-sized doll—
in clothes and high heels from our mothers' closets
and beads and baubles from our jewelry boxes.

Afterwards, our moms said folks were shocked
by Dougie's falsies and falsetto. When Doug said
he believed Jesus must have had a great laugh
and would have cracked up, our mothers surprised us
by agreeing. Then we all laughed like crazy,
as we did at some point during every Sunday dinner,
momentarily merry as Christmas—
laughter always our sweetest communion.

Stepfather

for Bruce

Poor Joseph has no clue
what he's gotten himself into.
Although his gaze is certain
as a hawk's, he cannot see
below the surface of this moment
when he claims the child,
palm open on his knee to support
the tiny feet, the other hand
over the belly to keep the standing
babe from falling over.

His headband tells me this time
Joseph is Apache, a gentle man
from a people turned warriors
by those who corralled them,
tried to steal their spirit.

I see you in this painting,
my blond Norwegian husband,
in the brave set of the face,
the tender hands. Jumping out
of airplanes with the 82nd airborne
must have looked, in retrospect,
like child's play next to raising
boys you hadn't fathered.

But you took them on
as more than mission,
although you couldn't see
the terrain where you'd be
landing, didn't know that
such a soldier wanders
a landmine-seeded desert,
that, looming over all, would be
a hazy figure who will
always be called Father.

✳

*from the painting of Joseph and the Christ Child
by Father John B. Giuliani (page 81)*

Father John B. Giuliani
Jesus and the Christ Child

Snow Globe

If my childhood had been colder,
I might not love the winter best
of all the seasons. If snow had not
been falling behind glass clouded
by the breath of supper cooking.
If I had not owned figure skates,
lived close enough to walk to the lagoon
that froze for Christmas break each year.
If the icy breeze had not been cracked
by giggling girls walking beside me,
skates slung like careless wings over our shoulders.

If I hadn't known myself so loved
that I could never die, I might have
been more shaky the first time
I trusted one lean blade to carry
all my young yearning for flight,
for beauty. Grandmother boasted

of a distant cousin who'd skated once
in the Olympics. Even her name—Matey—
was exotic as ice-glitter appearing
where just weeks before rough boys with Camels
hanging from curled lips had lowered
hooks into the dark water.

Even falling down, I wasn't scared
of going under. I was held up
by the watchful eyes of aunts
and mothers with faces smooth
as the ice before our blades sliced it.
Even in my cords and parka,
I was gliding toward their glamour,
ignoring the scrape of hockey sticks
when boys invaded. Already, I knew
the future owned me, just as winter
believes it owns the summer.

Miracles of All Shapes and Sizes

I.

Good things come in small packages
seemed a stupid saying to a girl
craving a baby doll for Christmas, even if I spied
Mom eyeing, with a bright surmise,
the jewelry box-sized package Dad placed under
the tree for her. Driving to our grandparents'
on Christmas Eve, Dad led his girls in *Silent Night*
and *Away in a Manger.* When we got to
O Little Town of Bethlehem, I marveled
at the dark streets of Omaha shining
with glittering lights on trees and houses,
and high above, *the everlasting light* of stars,
far away, I imagined, as Bethlehem and the birth
of the first Christmas. Grandmother's flocked tree
was the height of holiday glamor. As my sisters
and I passed out presents from beneath it,
I felt sorry for my parents, aunts, and uncles
who wouldn't be opening a single toy.
What could they possibly hope for?

II.

Two decades later, Christmas was a source
of worry, not wonder. How could I possibly
play Santa for my sons on my single mother's
tiny paycheck? Later, my mother called it
the Christmas God deposited cash in my account
because I was $200 over every time
I checked my balance that December.
Finally, I gave in to the glory of it,
ordering the cardboard teepee and clubhouse,
the walkie-talkie space helmets I'd heard them
exclaim over in the Christmas Wish Book.
The magic of it still catches in my throat
when I'm humming carols as I clean.
Especially this year, less than a month
after my beloved's—and their stepdad's—
late November death, when I discover in a drawer
of the oak desk I gave him, the bronze and green
enamel bracelet and earrings I'd admired
at the museum shop before his diagnosis—
a small box, its contents not so precious
by the world's standards, but to me
miraculous as gold carried to a manger
by a wise man from far, far away.

Madonna of the Wheat

I like Jesus better
when he's a helpless baby in your arms,
not this miniature dandy
in a red robe trimmed in gold,
arms outstretched as though
he would fly from you already.

Or does he extend his arms to bless
the field mice poised impossibly
on strands of golden wheat, front feet
waving hosannas, in this frame
where rodents replace angels?

Or he is a tiny host
spreading his arms in welcome,
bidding us partake of sheaves
climbing the sky, weaving
a veil between the dead and living.

Your russet hair reaches down
to enclose his halo. Your fingers
meeting at his waist are folded wings,
are praying. You must know
there is a seed ticking within him,
that there will be a harvest
and a grinding.

*

from the painting by Wieslawa Kwiatkowska

With My Mother in the Garden

Though you weren't into Mary,
you'd love these woodsy princesses
with long hair like your daughters'
when we were still your girls.
Whom do these girls belong to
with their peacock feather dresses,
cranberry-studded crowns,
bare feet even in winter?
To women like us, of course,
whose gardens are their chapels.

Mary's train is an entourage
of deer and bear and cougar,
and a flurry of herons, finches,
sparrows rises from the breeze
of her cape as she makes her way
between chrysanthemum and lily—
the simultaneous bursting
forth of seasons—in a garden
eternity has never fled.

It's the kind of place where
I'm always looking for you, sure
when you appear to one of us,
it will be where fur and petals,
wings and leaves are
always weaving this world
from the next one.

❋

*from the Polish Madonna oil paintings
of Wieslawa Kwiatkowska*

As It Is in Heaven

for Susan Williams Beckhorn

Going to church, my friend calls
her Sunday forest rambles.
Yet glimpsing my Nativity last Christmas,
Sue admitted craving one.
I savor such paradoxes—mysteries
like Jesus being *fully God and fully man.*

So when I happen on the Holy Family
and their entourage huddled between
die-cast soldiers and Kewpie dolls
at a roadside antiques mall a week
before Sue's solstice party, I don't know
what to call it—luck or grace.

Especially when I see the price
on a tag that also reads *as is.*
Searching for flaws, I caress
their silky porcelain contours,
discover the donkey's broken back,
inexpertly repaired, and one
Wise Man missing a thumb.

But I know she'll cherish
the sweet wonder of their faces
and forgive the imperfections
in this unlikely congregation of shepherds,
angels, kings, and barnyard beasts.

Like us around Sue's table, mostly unbelievers—
potters, bus drivers, professors, contractors,
divorced, disabled, and widowed—
finished with our turkey and watching her
unwrap each tissue-swaddled figure,
her fingers tender as when undressing
her babes before their baths deep in the past.

Oh, our murmurs and delighted sighs—
like children, starry-eyed, watching a pageant—
as she sets each one beside the others,
once again collapsing time to tell their story,
the one in which we're all *as is* and, in this moment
of shared awe, perfectly mended.

About the Author

photograph: Karl Schneider

Prize-winning poet Judith Sornberger is the author of three other full-length poetry collections—*I Call to You from Time* (Wipf & Stock, 2019), *Practicing the World* (CavanKerry, 2018) and *Open Heart* (Calyx Books)—and five chapbooks. Her prose memoir, *The Accidental Pilgrim: Finding God and His Mother in Tuscany*, is from Shanti Arts. She is professor emerita of Mansfield University of Pennsylvania where she taught English and created the Women's Studies Program. She lives on the side of a mountain outside Wellsboro, Pennsylvania, among deer, bears, and bobcats.

www.judithsornberger.net

SHANTI ARTS

NATURE ▪ ART ▪ SPIRIT

Please visit us online
to browse our entire book
catalog, including poetry
collections and fiction, books
on travel, nature, healing, art,
photography, and more.

Also take a look at our highly
regarded art and literary journal,
Still Point Arts Quarterly, which
may be downloaded for free.

WWW.SHANTIARTS.COM

www.ingramcontent.com/pod-product-compliance
Lightning Source LLC
Chambersburg PA
CBHW042047090426
42733CB00037B/2652